THIS
ROAD
SUCKS

AND OTHER STREET SIGNS WE REALLY NEED

Dan Consiglio and Brad DeMarea

RUNNING PRESS
PHILADELPHIA · LONDON

© 2014 by Dan Consiglio and Brad DeMarea
Published by Running Press,
A Member of the Perseus Books Group

Books published by Running Press are available at special discounts for bulk purchases in the United States by corporations, institutions, and other organizations. For more information, please contact the Special Markets Department at the Perseus Books Group, 2300 Chestnut Street, Suite 200, Philadelphia, PA 19103, or call (800) 810-4145, ext. 5000, or e-mail special.markets@perseusbooks.com.

ISBN 978-0-7624-5413-6
Library of Congress Control Number: 2013953190

9   8   7   6   5   4   3   2   1
Digit on the right indicates the number of this printing

Edited by Jordana Tusman
Typography: Futura

Running Press Book Publishers
2300 Chestnut Street
Philadelphia, PA 19103-4371

Visit us on the web!
www.runningpress.com

INTRODUCTION

America's complex network of highways, byways, side streets, alleys, and bumpy-as-shit back-ass country roads combine to create a pulsing nerve center for this enormous-as-fuck country. And to help keep America moving, it is imperative that each and every driver fully comprehends and obeys the rules of the road. *This Road Sucks* outlines important nationwide signage designed to keep drivers informed and aware of their surroundings.

Operating a motor vehicle, also known as "driving," or, in some cases, "straight-up rollin'," is a privilege, not a right. Whether you drive a car, a minivan, a truck with a gun rack and Jesus fish, a motorcycle, or a Shriner's car, the shared rules and responsibilities of the road are paramount to safe passage.

Please take the time necessary to commit each and every sign in this book to memory. Maybe try flashcards, moron. Remember, an informed driver is a safe driver.

Whether you are an elderly, experienced driver or a pimply-ass bitch who just earned your license, *This Road Sucks* is a must-read before you merge onto the road of life.

ASSHOLE AHEAD

Do not expect to be able to change lanes, because this asshole has no intention of letting you in. Driver should also be aware that it appears this asshole is wearing a scarf, listening to trance music, and downing a soy nonfat latte.

WORKMAN WITH THUMB UP ASS

Drivers may experience delays due to hungover and possibly stoned workmen standing around smoking and talking about poon they'll never get.

SHOCKINGLY FILTHY RESTROOM, NEXT EXIT

Be warned: The service station restroom has shit everywhere, and not just on the bowl. Somehow, there's even shit on the wall—and it's really high up there.

BUMP WILL FUCK UP YOUR CAR

Drivers, don't get all cute and try
to test this bump. This here bump means
fucking business.

STOPTIONAL

When this sign is present, drivers should recognize that the area is not currently policed and, let's be honest, never is because this block is so shitty. Proceed to roll through stops or ignore them altogether.

MOTEL THAT SHOWS PORN, NEXT EXIT

If driver feels an overwhelming urge to spank the frank, proceed to next exit for cheap motel with pay-TV porn.

LEFT BLINKER ON INDEFINITELY

Be aware that the mental giant
in front of you has no idea his left
turn signal has been on since the '80s.
Driver is allowed to casually flip
a bird as he or she passes
clueless fuck.

HIGHLY VISIBLE HORSE DONG

When this sign is present, motorists should prepare to see a two-foot* horse dong casually blowing in the breeze, urinating like a goddamn fire hose, searching out willing or unwilling horse poon, or simply getting some air.

*This is a conservative estimate.

SPEED ENFORCED BY AIRCRAFT (NOT REALLY)

Despite posting, this area is not really patrolled by aircraft. I mean, aircraft fitted with radar guns flying around just to monitor your speed? That's some dumb shit. At one time it seemed cool, but it just never panned out. Be warned that we are currently testing jetpacks strapped to police dogs.

SPEED ENFORCED BY AIRCRAFT
(NOT REALLY)

GO AHEAD AND FART, IT'S YOUR CAR

Drivers are allowed to freely and
legally pass noxious gas in their vehicles
when this sign is present. However,
drivers may face social repercussions
if they are not the owner of the car
in which they just cracked ass.

SPEED LIMIT 72, SERIOUSLY

Drivers are allowed to push the posted 65 mph speed limit to 72 mph max. Look, we're trying to be lenient here, but don't get all cute and push it to 75, because that frosts our ass, and we'll pull you over. Then we'll just sit in our car until the song on the radio has ended, and walk super slow up to your window just to waste your time.

SPEED LIMIT
72
SERIOUSLY

THIS STREET DARK
ENOUGH FOR SEX

Drivers are allowed to sink the
old battleship in marked areas.
Car must be parked, but radio may
be played softly. Consider cracking
the windows.

CAUTION: PARENTS ON CELL PHONES NOT GIVING A SOLITARY FUCK

When this sign is present, probability is high that there are parents on their cell phones talking, texting, Facebooking, and generally not giving a fuck about their wild-ass kids.

GOOD PLACE TO HIT THAT JAYWALKER

This is a minimally policed area. Drivers, if so willing, can bum-rush a jaywalker and send his or her ass flying.

NO PARKING WHEN SNOW IS OVER 2 INCHES (OR WE'LL PLOW YOUR ASS IN)

While we know that you can't control the amount of snowfall that may accrue when you are away from your legally parked vehicle—for, say, the eight hours you spend at work every goddamn day—just be aware, if flakes accrue more than two inches, we will plow your ass in.

NO PARKING WHEN SNOW IS OVER 2 INCHES OR WE'LL PLOW YOUR ASS IN

DRUNKEN HOBO SELLING YESTERDAY'S PAPER ON CORNER

When sign is present, drivers should raise all open windows immediately, or prepare for a blast of hot wino breath and stale urine that could make a eunuch wince.

LANE RESERVED FOR HIPSTERS ON FIXIES

This lane reserved for urban hipsters on fixed-wheel bicycles only. No old fatties on road bikes, techy nerds on scooters, or bus boys on cheap, imitation mountain bikes. Swerve into lane only where marked.

LANE RESERVED
FOR TRUCKERS WHO
WILL BONE ANYTHING.
AND WE MEAN
ANY-FUCKING-THING.

This lane only for horn-dog truckers
who will pork any toothless lot lizard
willing to climb into his or her
sweaty-ass cab.

ONLY

NEXT REST AREA 78 MILES, SO PISS IN A BOTTLE

There's no way around it: 78 miles is
a long way to hold your bladder,
especially for small children and old
people. To avoid wetting themselves and
staining vehicle upholstery, motorists
should consider pissing in a bottle.
Fast-food cups are not recommended, as
they will sweat—but shit, do what
you have to do.

NEXT REST AREA 78 MILES SO PISS IN A BOTTLE

WATCH FOR WHORES

Women of the night are known to frequent these premises. Drivers need be aware of scantily clad ladies offering hoovers, old-fashioneds, and Boston shockers for monetary gain. Prices may vary and are negotiable. Repeat: negotiable.

JUST DON'T EVER FUCKING PARK HERE, OK?

Drivers should not even consider parking here. We could post all the dozens of restrictions, but when we added all the shit up, you could only legally park here at 3:17AM on the second Tuesday of every other month. See what we mean?

MILEAGE SIGN

Six miles to depressing, once-proud
farms; seventeen miles to know-it-all
rednecks who've never left this town;
thirty-two miles to dangerous low-grade
meth produced in a cockroach-
infested trailer by a tatted-up, ex-con
named Zach.

Farms	**6**
Rednecks	**17**
Meth	**32**

DEAD SKUNCOONOSSUMILLO ON ROAD

Watch for dead skuncoonossumillo in road. We honestly don't know what the fuck that thing was, but it's split in half now.

NEXT RIGHT:
GAS, FOOD, PHONE,
AND LIKE 12 ADULT
SUPERSTORES

At the next posted exit, drivers
will find fuel stations, food, pay phones,
and more porn than you can shake
a blue dildo at.

BRIDGE MAY BE MORE SLIPPERY THAN A WITCH'S TIT

"Slippery when wet" did not get the message across. After all, it's a pretty soft sell, so we amped shit up a bit. We don't really understand what the whole "witch's tit" reference means, yet in focus groups it really got the point across. Proceed with caution.

WARNING:
FERAL DOG FUCK FEST

Primarily in southern border regions
and near customs checkpoints,
motorists should be prepared for canine
bone fests that will blow their minds.
Feral dogs in these areas frequently
screw smack-dab in the middle of the
streets after consuming poorly hidden
bags of cocaine. Strap in.

WARNING

DO NOT BLOCK DRIVEWAY BECAUSE IT'S NOT YOUR GODDAMN DRIVEWAY

When driver buys this house and the driveway referenced by posted sign becomes driver's driveway, then driver can block it all-the-goddamn-day-long. Until such events pass, stop eyeing that spot like the old creep who sits alone at the college bar, and move along.

NO PARKING

DO NOT BLOCK DRIVEWAY

WHY DOES THIS
EVEN NEED A SIGN?
IS THIS YOUR
DRIVEWAY? NO? KEEP
LOOKING, JERK.

STUPID ROUNDABOUT
UP AHEAD

Drivers should prepare for a cute little roundabout thingy that makes no fucking sense whatsoever. It's just us trying to be a little cheeky and British, even though we all know that shit doesn't work over here.

WHAT THE
FUCK?

SLOW(ISH)

When sign is posted, motorists should
proceed slow-ish. We're not saying
you have to really hit the brakes, but
a lot of the turtleneck-and-khaki-wearing
parents in this neighborhood have
complained, and, frankly, we're sick
of hearing their shit.

WATCH FOR HOT, FOREIGN NANNIES WITH NAMES LIKE ANJA

Drivers, you know what we're talking about. Don't even play.

HISTORIC DOWNTOWN WITH ABSOLUTELY NOTHING WORTH SEEING

In fact, it only gets a sign because this town is old as shit. It smells like farts because of the fertilizer plant they dropped in where the high school used to be, and it's rumored that the river causes cancer.

HISTORIC
DOWNTOWN

WITH ABSOLUTELY
NOTHING WORTH
SEEING

THAT'S RIGHT—IT'S A FUCKING AIRPORT!

Drivers and passengers should immediately stop staring open-mouthed at the sky like they've just witnessed the invention of fire. Those "flying machines" are called airplanes. Now get your eyes on the road before you rear-end the befuddled sky-gazer in front of you and fuck up traffic for the rest of us.

AIRPORT

ACT LIKE YOU'VE
SEEN A FUCKING
PLANE BEFORE

SICKLY COWS OFF HIGHWAY

Shield your eyes, drivers. Area cows have been injected with more HGH than the Oakland A's of the '80s. These milkers are so fucking strung out and used up they can't give an ounce of dust.

RESTROOM WITH GLORY HOLE AHEAD

Restroom at next exit contains at least one glory hole. We can't speak to the level of activity or sexual orientation most frequently exhibited at said G-hole, but then again, it's pretty much about the surprise, right fellas? Enjoy!

PARKING AVAILABLE NEAR PIGEONS THAT EAT INDIAN FOOD OUT OF THE GARBAGE

Parking allowed here as long as driver has really thought this through. If you think Indian food fucks you up, imagine what a good spicy curry does to the digestive system of a sorry-ass pigeon.

LEFT LANE CLOSED AHEAD, TIME TO DRIVE LIKE A DICK

Be warned that the marked lane
will be closed to traffic in 500 feet.
That gives you 499 feet to pass all the
grandmas, college nerds, and white
trashies you can. Go!

TIME TO SPREAD THE SHIT AROUND. NO PARKING.

No one knows why this little butt-plug of a vehicle from 1960 has never been improved upon, but until it is, we will continue to spread the shit around to different parts of the street on the third Wednesday of each month from 9AM to 11AM. Weather permitting.

SPREADING THE
SHIT AROUND TO
DIFFERENT PARTS
OF THE STREET
9AM – 11AM
3RD WEDNESDAY
OF THE MONTH

TOW ZONE

GODDAMN FLY IN CAR

Drivers should recognize that there's a goddamn fly in the car. Drivers can try cracking a window to see if the fly will "get the hell out of here," but flies are pretty stupid and that doesn't always work. Do not slap wildly at fly like a one-armed, retarded bear.

BOARD FOUL BUS HERE

Pedestrians may board city buses
at marked locations. Be warned that
these buses are not equipped with
restrooms and, from time to time, small
puddles of urine will pool up on the
floor. We're not sure who's to blame
for this, but we're really upset about it.
Not upset enough to do anything,
but upset nonetheless.

BUS STOP

BOARD HERE
FOR A WHIFF
OF THE FAINT
BUT PUNGENT
SCENT OF URINE

SHITTY STATE PARK

We're as shocked as you are that
this half-acre dump with four 1970s
barbecue pits is classified as a
state park. Oh well, have at it; no one
polices this hole anyway.

THEY ACTUALLY
REFER TO THIS
DUMP AS A
STATE PARK?

OK TO UNBUTTON TOP BUTTON

In areas where sign is present, it is OK for drivers to unbutton the old governor of the waistband. Maybe even a couple notches on the zipper, but let's not get carried away.

PEOPLE IN THIS TOWN
WEAR OVERALLS

The residents of this ass-fuck backward
town still wear overalls. Motorists
are advised not to focus on the ample,
highly visible white meat gathering
under the rancid denim.

WATCH FOR FATTIES IN BIKE SHORTS

Motorists should be on the lookout for older men squeezed into expensive cycling gear, resembling sausage casings on wheels. These old farts take this shit seriously: Watch for overly theatrical hand signals.

ONE WAY, UNLESS DRUNK

Drivers can only proceed in direction of arrow, unless they are drunk. Then whatever the fuck goes.

ONE
WAY

→

UNLESS DRUNK

PAVEMENT SMOOTH AS A BABY'S ASS

This is a wealthy neighborhood—
didn't you see the Aryan youth playing
lacrosse? Be prepared for silky-smooth
road conditions, not like that bumpy
shit in your hood.

MAN DIGGING FOR GOLD

Drivers be warned that the old prospector in the next lane has his finger so far up his schnoz it appears to be massaging his brain.

REST AREA HASN'T BEEN UPDATED SINCE 1971

Need a rotary phone, coffee vending machine, inaccurate road map, or a space-age, tree-mounted can crusher? Coming up!

REST AREA

HASN'T BEEN UPDATED
SINCE 1971

TOTALLY FUCKED TRUCK

Warning: That truck is totally
fucked. Do not help truck. Let it go.
Truck got himself into this mess,
and now truck has to get himself
out of it.

TAKE ANY ROUTE, JUST GET THE HELL OUT OF THIS RACIST, CRACKER-ASS TOWN

This town makes the one from *Deliverance* feel like San Francisco. Drivers should find the nearest direct route out as fast as fucking possible. Ol' Wilbur and Jackie Boy are fixin' to take their gimp out for a walk.

WARNING:
FUZZ SLEEPING

Drivers should take notice of
their tax dollars hard at work while
Johnny Law takes a siesta after
lunchtime burritos and on-duty beers.
Code ZZZ!

RESERVED PARKING
FOR EXPECTANT MOTHERS
OR TOTAL ASSHOLES

Do not park in marked area unless
another human is visibly growing inside
your stomach and you are beginning to
feel discomfort as you hoist your newly
widened load out of the car. Total
and complete assholes may also
park in marked area, even if it's for the
whole day.

RESERVED
PARKING

FOR
EXPECTANT
MOTHERS
OR TOTAL ASSHOLES

ENTERING AMISH COMMUNITY THAT HAS PRETTY MUCH GIVEN UP

Do not be alarmed by mangy-ass donkeys pulling rickety carts. What used to be a quaint Amish community known for its quality unpainted furniture is now nothing more than a couple of beardies holding up traffic.

FLAGGER AHEAD. OR POSSIBLY MAN HOLDING BAG OF SHIT?

Drivers should be prepared for a flagger ahead. But honestly, the art department really fucked this one, and it could just as easily be a man holding a smelly bag of shit at arm's length. Do what you will.

CHARMING FRUIT STAND SELLING PESTICIDE-LADEN FRUIT UP AHEAD

Motorists and pedestrians should not be fooled by the cute, young blonde in cutoffs or the letterpressed logo featuring a smiling dumb-ass rabbit; that fruit has more chemicals in it than Jacko's corpse.

CAUTION: MAN
ATTEMPTING TO MAKE
EYE CONTACT WITH
ANYTHING THAT HAS
A PAIR OF TITS

Female and transgender motorists
should be prepared for unwanted stares
from losers—and possibly virgins—in
imitation sports cars.

DETOUR. OH SHIT.

You are correct, driver, it's a fucking detour. Follow impossibly marked, basically homemade signs through small towns and cornfields to the exact wrong location with no cell coverage. See you later!

OH SHIT

BUCKLE UP! WHEN PULLED OVER

Motorists should be warned that lazy, quota-hungry pigs will pull your ass over for nothing more than employing a late turn signal, then tack on an extra hundo in fines if your seat belt isn't buckled.

BUCKLE UP!

WHEN PULLED OVER

YIELD TO STRAPPED NUTJOBS

In marked areas, drivers should
yield to fully strapped loners with
crazy eyes and military jackets.
Do not yell "fuck you!", flip the bird,
or sarcastically mimic a hand job
unless expertly trained in duck
and cover.

BIG-ASS SODAS, NEXT EXIT

Take the next exit for 64-ounce, big-ass sodas, perfect for a thirsty redneck like yourself. And as long as you're going through the trouble of hauling your XXXL self out of the sagging cab of that pickup, you might as well grab one for that big-boned gal you've been bangin'.

SEEMINGLY NORMAL TOLLBOOTH ATTENDANT, RIGHT LANE

We're as blown away as you are, but it appears the tollbooth attendant in the right lane might not be totally insane. Do not talk with seemingly normal attendant, however. Because, as we all know, sitting in a tollbooth all day makes you crazier than a shithouse rat.

TOLL PLAZA

NORMAL
ATTENDANT
RIGHT LANE

SUPREMELY ARROGANT DEER ABOUT TO BE TAKEN DOWN A NOTCH

Drivers are free to marvel at majestic-as-fuck deer as a delivery truck explodes his cocky ass into road dust.

QUIZ

Before attempting to tackle the open road, make sure you're "up to speed" on the signs in this book and that you really know what all this shit means. Here's a quick quiz to test your knowledge:

1. Regulation signs may contain illustrations of animal schlongs, but not sphincters, tight or relaxed. True or false?

2. What color sign signals a highly regarded prostitute in the vicinity?

3. Inside a work zone marked by orange signage, it's OK for a workman to piss behind large machinery like a backhoe or steamroller, as long as it's not where everyone eats lunch. True or false?

4. Do police really monitor your speed by aircraft, or is that just some *Jetson*-type bullshit that sounded cool after a couple beers?

5. It is OK to flip the bird at hippies in low-power hybrids occupying the fast lane. True or false?

6. Assholes may park in spots marked for expectant mothers only if they're stopping in to purchase smokes or a bag of jerky. True or false?

7. Pets may drive if they have obtained legal operator permits. True or false?

8. Drivers may unbutton the top button of their pants:
   A) in marked areas   B) from sundown to sun up
   C) after burritos   D) at party time

9. Drivers may roll through or straight-up blow a stop sign if Johnny Law is nowhere in sight. True or false?

10. A sign depicting a man with a finger way up his nose signifies:
    A) everyone, smell your finger   B) driver digging for gold
    C) something is really lodged up there

Answers on next page.

ANSWERS

1. False. Schlongs and tight sphincters are depicted in road signs.
2. Yellow.
3. True.
4. It's clearly *Jetson*-type bullshit.
5. True. A bird flip or mock bj is acceptable.
6. False. Assholes may also purchase pornomags and schnapps.
7. False. Jesus, pay attention.
8. D. Because party time is whenever you want it to be, bitches.
9. True.
10. B. Although the other options are good ones, too.